ld Tree

Pitt Poetry Series
Ed Ochester, Editor

World Tree

DAVID WOJAHN

University of Pittsburgh Press

Published by the University of Pittsburgh Press, Pittsburgh, PA 15260

Copyright © 2011, David Wojahn

Manufactured in the United States of America

Printed on acid-free paper

10 9 8 7 6 5 4 3 2 1

ISBN 13: 978-0-8229-6142-0

ISBN 10: 0-8229-6142-3

For Noelle, Jake, and Luke

and for William Olsen
David Jauss
Tony Whedon

There was a young man came to me in my dream.
Bearded, wearing a headdress. He carried a tablet.

And on the tablet written was a message:
"Marduk has sent me. I come to bring you luck.

To Shubshi-meshre-Shakkan I bring good luck."
The storm of Marduk's anger was quieted down.

A lion was eating me. Marduk muzzled the lion.
Marduk took my hand and raised me up.

He who had thrown me down he raised me up.
My knees, which were fettered and bound like the busu-bird's,

My knees were freed from my bonds and I could walk.

My throat, which was closed, was opened, and I sang.

—from *Shubshi-meshre-Shakkan*, trans. David Ferry

CONTENTS

Scribal: My Mother in the Voting Booth

Stabbing the hole by Nixon's name, with a stylus on a chain,
    like some scribe
in Lagash piercing wet clay slabs for the palace records. The count
    for the priest king's
chariots & Amorite slaves must be exact. All day her adding machine
    has purred, the shavings

litter the floor. Stylus through Nixon, stylus through Agnew. Two hours
    she's waited in the wet
November snow of Minnesota & her cold next week will worsen
    to pneumonia. Over
the churning columns she'll cough & pass out & waken in County General,
    shrouded in an oxygen tent

where she cannot smoke. The count must be exact—14 lyres with
    the heads of bearded bulls,
130 votives, 6 figurines of Marduk fashioned of hammered gold.
    The water glass is trembling.
Beside her bed I hover, the clear walls of the tent breathe in & out.
    Flicker of Cronkite,

of Nixon on the wall in black & white. He has a secret plan
    to end the war.
She sleeps. The tent draws a breath & the joint I smoked
    in the parking lot turns the light
a jack-o'-lantern orange. I tell myself in my teenage hubris
    that I will not work on

Maggie's Farm like her. Ain't gonna work like her
    to blindly serve.
But how her white ectoplasmic face looms back at me this morning
    (breathe in, breathe out,
the tent's rise & fall) in the waiting room of Richmond Pediatrics.
    All night Luke's coughed,

meaning the pneumonia's returned & the office radio oozes hate,
  talk show & its porcine
fascist droning on. He has a secret plan to replace the Constitution
  with gelignite.
Over us all it washes, the fine volcanic dust, over the fevered
  toddlers of the suburbs

& their mothers in sensible shoes, over the *Parenting*s
  & *Mademoiselle*s
& the parking lot minivans, the toxic "W"s affixed to their bumpers.
  Breathe in & serve
breathe in & serve. A slab of plastic for the co-pay,
  the computer station hums.

Cylinder seal & tapestry, ninety geldings in the palace stables. Nebulizer
  spewing Pulmicort.
Pink amoxicillin, doctored to taste like bubblegum. seven double-headed
  battleaxes, burnished bronze
now oxidized the color of pond scum. Blindly, blindly do we serve.
  O Priest King, Dear Leader,

Jealous God. There hangs her scarlet car coat with its Nixon button,
  bogus leopard skin along the collar.
She unzips the tent, she recovers. Manhattans prohibited for fourteen days.
  The adding machine reanimates,
numbers coughing & the tapes scrolling out. She lives on, twenty more
  deluded years. In the parking lot,

Rx in hand, I strap sleeping Luke in his car seat—streetlights, the yellow
  & blood-red leaves, pasted
to the window by the rain. Let me serve him. Let me live on
  twenty years. Let me stand
above the burial pits, their goods interred & catalogued, the miles
  of dirt tamped down.

August, 1953

A nurse gathers up the afterbirth. My mother

had been howling but now could sleep.

By this time I am gone—also gathered up

& wheeled out. Above my jaundiced face the nurses hover.

Outside, a scab commands a city bus. The picketers battle cops

& ten thousand Soviet conscripts in goggles

kneel & cover their eyes. Mushroom cloud above the Gobi,

& slithering toward Stalin's brain, the blood clot

takes its time. Ethel Rosenberg has rocketed

to the afterlife, her hair shooting flame. The afterbirth

is sloshing in a pail, steadied by an orderly who curses

when the elevator doors stay shut: I am soul & body & medical waste

foaming to the sewers of St. Paul. I am not yet aware

of gratitude or shame.
                    I do know the light is everywhere.

Screensaver: Pharaoh

We had eaten the placenta in a soup that someone based on a family recipe
      for menudo, though someone else—
it was Bill, I think—joked that it tasted just like chicken. *This Year's Model*
      was brand new & the needle stuck
on "Lipstick Vogue," Costello snarling *not just another mouth, not just*
      another mouth, until Joe

set down the bong & flicked the tone arm forward from the scratch.
      & anyway, by this time
Amy was shouting from the bedroom that she'd finally gotten Star to sleep,
      that the music should be
Mozart or something. I've forgotten the midwife's name, but she sat
      sprawled on a patio chair,

the distant blink of Tucson down the mountainside. She held an iced Corona
      & told us she was too worn-out
to drive the snaking foothill two-lanes home. Good dope, cheap champagne,
      a soup of afterbirth:
everybody but the midwife garrulous & now Papageno was flapping
      birdman wings in his mating dance

around fair Papagena. So the talk turned to duets—scholastic in the way
      that stoner conversations go.
Whose placenta was it we slurped down with cilantro & a dash of cumin,
      telling ourselves the taste
was not half bad—Amy's or Star's? & what about Derek, who now
      had moved to Mykonos,

leaving his storied seed behind: what portion of the recipe was owed
      to him? Now came the tricky part—
where did the soul inhere? The midwife rimmed her longneck with
      a lemon slice & allowed
that we'd ingested perfection, the body's all-in-one: liver, kidney,
      blood supply,

its vascular estuaries spidering from delta to sea, tasting not just of flesh,
     but of the corpus entire,
which we all agreed was pretty far-out. Lord how I yearn sometimes
     for those days of sudden
bedazzling insight, however false & addled. My eyes went Blakean.
     By the firelight I watched

the quaking dance of souls, bi- & tri- & quadrifurcated & hovering among us
     in a pea-soup fog,
lavish as dry ice a-swirl from a spliff. My soul, your soul, our soul.
     The Oversoul broadcasting
its hundred thousand watts of Motown to the radio speakers of the whole
     Southwest; Aretha Soul & Otis Soul

& Sam Cooke Soul. & Pneuma, weighing twenty grams of blazing light.
     But then the tone arm
reached the aria's end. The LP clicked off. The room became
     sleeping bags & pillows,
Mexican blanket covering a ratty sofa. The parts we didn't eat
     we double-bagged

& carried to the dumpster, padlocked to confound the coyotes.
     The midwife took the couch
& slept. & by the firelight the whole clan slumbered, the cave wall
     throwing shadows. This was
thirty years ago. Where the business of the world has taken us
     I cannot say. I reboot,

the pixels gather themselves & pulse at me. I could Google Amy,
     Google Star, MapQuest
Speedway Boulevard & call up Derek's obit from the *Sentinel*.
     But the screen instead
coalesces to a tomb painting of Pharaoh. Lordly he walks,
     preceded by his vassals,

who bear his emblems & trophies, hoisted atop tall staffs.
     Among them

is Pharaoh's placenta, preserved & flapping like an ensign.
        Raised to the sky,
the crimson portal hovers in the wind. From it the God-King
        fell headfirst into this world.

Ending with a Quotation from *Walden*

For three generations
            their farmlands
                        withered
& the Anasazi
            took to eating human flesh,
                        their enemies
First, then at last
            their kinsmen.
                        A pattern
Of scored
            & incised human bones
                        is evidence,
If you know how
            to read the auguries
                        of microscopes.
Forensic:
            from the Latin *forensis,*
                        the marketplace.
The forum
            where debate was engaged,
                        where tricks
Of rhetoric & gesture
            might enhance
                        your case.
But so much
            is conjecture—
                        whose sad flesh
Was churned within
            this white-ware pot?
                        Stranger
Or kin?
        The Hated One?
                    The Beloved One whose touch
You'd stir to
        in the dawn,

now portioned & shared

In ghostly ritual?

Or did you sunder bone

between your teeth

& gloating, ingest

the marrow of

your foe?

The innermost:

I wanted to live deep,

writes Thoreau,

& suck out

all the marrow

of this life.

Nazim

Perched with the chainsaw on the branch, he bends toward the trunk
     as the others cry *loco* & the sawdust
fizzes toward his goggles, the engine seething & just when the branch begins
     to sway & creak he's got
the motor off, earthbound again & chugging Gatorade, my twins
     at the window, spellbound.

The hurricane's left downed trees for miles, power lines still tentacling the streets
     though it's been weeks since
the eye passed over. Our crew's all Mexican save for him—Nazim from Istanbul,
     whose namesake, he tells me,
is Hikmet the Poet. "They locked him in our prisons for years, Professor.
     They didn't like Reds."

He hands the empty jug to me, stubbing a cigarette & grinning at the boys.
     Because his English is better
than his Spanish, he talks with me while the others lunch. They have christened him,
     el turco, el turco loco,
who steeplejacks the trunks in a manic dervish. They've been at it for days,
     the felled oaks neatly stacked

in rows where the shed had been. The cherry pickers of Dominion Power
     hover the streets & the boys
have learned to shout *hola* at spoons & neighborhood cats, at newel posts
     & themselves & Nazim's
shown me pictures—the wife & daughters waiting in Istanbul, by the turbid briny
     Bosporus Hikmet smelled but couldn't view

from the window by the ceiling of his cell. The boys prowl the living room,
     shirtless in the heat,
a crescent moon of scar on Jake's right side, where they pried
     his dead kidney from him
at six months; the jagged white skin glistens. Yesterday, Nazim pulled his T-shirt up
     for Carlos & Pepe to view

the zigzag handiwork of his own operation, a kidney sold in Israel,
      $4,000 American,
enough for passage to Miami where a brother, praise Allah, waited.
      He joked about
the hospital food, kosher but not half-bad. Three years since he's seen his family
      & maybe three years more

before he'll have the cash to send for them. "Not easy to wait that long,"
      he tells me, "but possible.
Look at Hikmet." Thirteen years of prison, thirteen more of exile, dying in Moscow
      on a day of wet spring snow:
How will they get me down from the third floor? he worried in a poem.
      The coffin won't fit the elevator,

& the stairs are so narrow. Again he pulls the photo from his wallet,
      giving thanks, even to the Brazilian
who owns his kidney, which rides a limo through the boulevards of Rio
      & daily rubs against
a money belt thick with bills & floats beside a bladder streaming piss
      into a marble urinal,

its gold-plated fixtures agleam. Praise Allah, as if justice & injustice could be
      equally miraculous
& both as blissfully blind. Praise Mammon, Tribute & Elohim,
      Praise Storm God
& the sultry Muse of Dialectical Materialism, Her earnest luster faded.
      Nazim wipes his brow;

the air reeks of gasoline & in a penthouse by the Sugarloaf
      a scowl with sunglasses
checks a beeper, orders barked into his cell. In Istanbul a woman wakes alone
      at dawn to pack lunch
for her daughters to carry to school & in the poem a girl in Oakland reads,
      Hikmet still rides the train

from Prague to Berlin, March 28, 1962, lighting his sixth cigarette
      & listing the things

he didn't know he loved, among them clouds & rain & engine sparks.
    The boys knock down
a Lego castle as the lights blaze on for the first time in weeks,
    the microwave beeping,

TV flaring up with a nattering soap. They're at the screen door
    shouting *hola*
as the chainsaws set themselves upon the last downed oak, the crew
    intoning *turco loco,*
while Nazim teeters on a limb he cuts half-through before
    he leaps back earthward.

Christet at Emmaus

> *Craquelure*—the fine pattern of cracks formed on old paintings. It is sometimes used to detect forged art, as craquelure is a hard-to-forge signature of authenticity.

Now they recognize that He's the Risen One, something in His gesture
    as he breaks the bread,
& the light as it plays through the glass, backlit by the dying sun,
    His eyes closed for the blessing.
He is clothed in ultramarine, color-of-far-across-the-sea.
    The serving plate & flagons

shimmer in the honeyed light. The tablecloth flares a dazzling whiteness,
    though uncanny questions
& sorrowful mysteries remain. Not that He soon shall vanish,
    not that their hearts
should burn within them as He talks, but how stiffly they pose beside Him;
    the hand of Peter is a lifeless prop

& the serving woman's eyes are saucers, a treacly half-smile on her face.
    Beyond the gilded frame,
it is 1938. Chamberlain with his shut umbrella steps off the plane
    from Munich, waving his scrap
of worthless treaty. Lindbergh poses with Goering in the cockpit
    of a Junkers 88, grinning

for the camera, his newly bestowed medal agleam. A studio doctor
    taps on Judy Garland's arm
to find a vein—Methedrine & B-12, so her dance with the Tin Man
    may continue. Frida Kahlo
spits out Trotsky's come into a washbasin of hammered tin.
    Nanking smolders; Barcelona falls,

but here at the Museum Boymans, a lost Vermeer's unveiled.
    The barbarous world
of signs & wonders has been barred at the door, replaced by *Holland:*
    Four Centuries of Masterworks.

Opening night, & the crowd seethes around the risen savior.
From London, New York

& Buenos Aires, the critics have thronged. They compete
for superlatives;
they jostle for a better view & a tall dapper man, pencil-mustached,
waits his turn for his audience
with God. He is Han van Meegeren, though he himself is God
the Father, who begot His Risen Son

from a badly rendered *Raising of Lazarus*, seventeenth century, purchased at auction
for 1,400 guilders.
Three hundred years the dead man staggered from his tomb, only to be scraped
unceremoniously
from his canvas, meticulously as flaying. Wormhole, foxmark,
tabula rasa, the canvas now Malevich plain.

After eight bogus Halses & three ter Borches, he is ready to begin,
paint mixed with lavender
& lilac oil, & a foul-smelling plastic from America—Bakelite.
He saws the canvas down
to make it fit his oven. In a chair by the oven door, he sips schnapps
& waits for the cracks

to spider the window, the tablecloth, the luminous bread that pearls
with sunshine—craquelure.
& this time the recipe's correct. Now the second act commences,
papers falsified,
the provenance rigged, the usual story of desperate Jews
selling their birthrights

for passage to New York, the experts stunned before
"the greatest Vermeer of all."
Van Meegeren shoulders through the crowd. He stands before
his graven carnage,
his hypocrite double, his twin in purple robes, who will watch
the smokestacks

cinder the skies, & all the cites of the plain flare up in the night
        with their chemical sheen,
the beaches running red. He will watch & wait.
        Craquelure—
broadcast like radio waves, over the quadrants & the steppes,
        the atolls & the shtetls

& the blazing chancelleries. A dazzling whiteness. Van Meegeren
        pockets his pince-nez
& turns for home. The twenty-seven photojournalists are now
        permitted their moment;
they kneel, stand & crouch. Almost in unison, the cameras crackle,
        a writhing & enraptured light.

For the Honorable Wayne LaPierre, President,
National Rifle Association

Someone filed off the serial number of the Glock. Someone bought it
        & sold it & someone else
sold it again & thus Howard Reed Scott III, 17, shot Tyler Binsted,
        19, by the tennis courts in Byrd Park,
1 a.m. on a rainy Thursday, a robbery gone afoul. You were asleep
        in beltway Maryland then,

a "gated community," security alarm enabled, your own handgun loaded
        in the bedside table drawer.
Deeply you slept, having all day submitted to reporters' questions
        after the High Court overturned
the DC handgun ban. The Second Amendment once again preserved,
        a victory not just for the NRA,

but for all freedom-loving Americans. Deeply you slept as Tyler Binsted
        bled out against
the tennis court fence, as Howard Reed Scott hurled the Glock
        to the freeway roadside
from the window of his girlfriend's car. You had read until you drifted off,
        your wife beside you slumbering.

I do not know what book you closed, but assume it was not Dante,
        who places the violent
In hell's Seventh Circle, Second Ring. Dante also was a politician,
        though an unsuccessful one,
dying poor & in exile. I will not bore you with the partisan quarrels
        of Dante's Florence, of Guelph

against Ghibelline, of house arrest & banishment. But I can tell you
        Circle Seven is a river of blood,
where Dante situates Alexander, Attila & various tyrants, those whose
        violence to others
brings down cities & nations. The river, furthermore, is boiling,
        darkly crimson in the stygian reaches,

lit from afar by plains of fire. The damned cannot rise above
     the singeing waters.
Pushed down into the bloody depths by the centaurs who guard them,
     they cannot speak
to bewail their condition. I do not know you, Sir. Tyler Binsted
     & Howard Reed Scott

are surely unknown names to you, & if they were known,
     would be quickly forgotten.
I cannot read Italian & my art is limited & clumsy. But Dante,
     I am convinced,
would place you in the depths of Phlegethon, his boiling crimson river.
     He would make your pain unbearable;

forever the seething blood would scorch & fill your lungs.
     Dante Alighieri
was a man of peace, though famously self-righteous, aggressive,
     flawed. Yet many & eloquent
were his statements on freedom. He believed some sins could be forgiven.
     Regarding others, he was pitiless.

Self-Portrait Photo of Rimbaud with Folded Arms:
Abyssinia, 1883

To be already your own ghost, to be weak light a-slither,

somebody else in sandals, as if folding your arms

could keep you anchored to this planet. Pilgrim, stranger,

face a latticework of shadow. The banana tree in sepia flames

above your shoulder, the whole composition "too white,"

overexposed, "plates washed in this country's

bad water." Somebody else, simulacrum, *khat*

& hearth smoke, midday sun of August & no breeze.

Your gunrunner squint: revenant self to also be erased,

leaving nothing but account books, tallying the sales of slaves.

Piss on logos, tourniquet & syllables which cannot salve

your ache, leg irons for captives, last suppers for ghosts.

Alchemize silence. Alchemize fever. Gangrenous logos:

cut it with a bone saw but the phantom pain goes on.

Rolltop

Where she wrote a last book & I
      write now, coming apart again,
            though several times nailed steady.

The Lebus Desk: inscripted with tarnish
      at the keyhole & the slats coiling
            up as the lock uncatches. (Singe

of patchouli in memory, murk of a junk shop
      off Fullerton.) Brand name
            un-Googleable, though her own name

pulses from the pitchblende screens
      anew, her poems in print again.
            Oakstained, whorled, scrimshawed with

the verdigris of sweat & fingertip,
      you must have memorized her face
            staring down, eyeglass glint & the mottle

of the notebook covers where the words
      issued forth to be slashed out.
            & you placid, surface finessed to verb,

the language schooling silver beneath
      your hull & she so fearful
            & enraptured of this netting. How far

from shore she ventured with you,
      provisioned with gooseneck, nerve end,
            Chet Baker, Miles. Reluctant matter

gathered, Rx pad, dollhead trepanned,
      travel alarm spitting out its minutes
            by the photographs, the unutterable

secret alphabets hammered to clarity.
        She switches on the lamp, keyhole
                jimmied & I open, fingers with their bitten

nails, tapping then stroking my each
        knot & pitted whorl. Her eyes
                upon me, the stare ferocious & the whiteness

incised with its portion of me, resinous
        & maculate. No longer am I adrift.
        Lebus, I am very much not

your dear last master, but let my
        touch be as hers, let the language
                use us well. Above you my hand

now hovers. I take up the resting pen.

      —*after W. S. Graham*

Napping on My Fifty-Third Birthday

Middle or late,
        we cannot know.
                We spoon like children,
purple throw scattered
        & your mystery rustling
                open on the bed,
In Haifa, a bomb crater,
        dog-eared in a magazine.
                Here,
the ceiling fan's thrum.
        Here, John Clare
                has been searching
a yellowhammer's nest
        for the holy, embers
                from the Gypsy camps,
his madness a decade away
        & thus *the place*
                we occupy
seems all the world.
        Salt-rinsed,
                we have moored
once more at Ithaca,
        the heat finally broken,
                the last
hydrangeas
        bowing blossoms to the lawn,
                azure
transfigured back to gray,
        spent flashbulbs
                the shade of old letters,
par avion,
        reread until the creases
                softly tear

& wedged into
  some attic suitcase,
          your dead & mine,
the shades who each year grow
          less hungry & insistent,
                  their speech
now trenchant,
      picked clean.
          Down the upstairs hall
the boys sigh in dream;
      the red arc of the monitor
              ripples & quiets.
With pulleys & cherry pickers,
          chainsaws slurring,
                  the workers ease
the neighbors'
      dead oak groundward,
              a system strangely cantilevered,
like those stage devices
      built to raise
          & lower gods.
Eyes closed, you turn to me.
          I stroke your sleeping face.
                  Clare
sets homeward from Essex Asylum,
          perilous & long
                  the journey,
o summer pleasures
      they are gone.
          Noiseless, the oak tree
meets the ground.
      The chainsaws begin their dividing,
              sawdust smell,
the sibilant wail,
      the twenty-seven synonyms for blue.
                  Grant me this life,

thou spirit of the shades,
                         this place
                                    we occupy, this instant
indivisible.
             Ripple & quiet, pulley & chain,
                                        your eyes cleave open.

Quicken

—After a line by WCW

From the vast oceanic rocking, from the turbid
depths in which
        all night the currents

lave us shoreward, from some confounding
one with this ebb & flow of world,
                o we now are beached

& dream recedes back to its amniotic
bathyal zones. Now we are cold & brine-drenched,

mosaic that was our breathing riven apart,
crushed to beach glass,
          catching the eye of a child

& hurled back down, too jagged & uncolorful to hoard.
But then in your arms I startle awake, all present tense

& my oneness with you remakes the world.
5 a.m. Our touching is electric,
            flung silk & a new breath

that quickens us to fingertip, tumescence, thrall.
The new world naked
       & all its honeyed salt.

Fetish Value

The term my friend used yesterday, explaining
    Why the book can never disappear.
        The bar was smoky, nearing last call,

A techno-zealot colleague baiting him
    Over a pitcher of foamy Yuengling, under
        The widescreen flicker of Iceland besting Serbia

At soccer. The crowd went wild in Reykjavik
    & my friend grew fierce: always hands will yearn
        To still the flutter of the pages' susurration

In summer beneath a ceiling fan; always a woman
    Will gather the bundled cloth & ivory paper
        In her hands, the lamplight circling just so.

Lickerish the feeling. She positions herself;
    The tongue wets the right finger, so the page
        May be caressed before it's turned, lavish

Spillage, constant incunabulum. Garamond,
    Bodoni, Treadweave & Kennerly,
        Faint rough music of indentation brailing

& brailing the leaves. Always the tongue
    To draw the lips into an insistent
        Corporeal *o* & I thought of you, Aleda,

The big hair & the laugh that would reduce
    This whole vast enterprise of pedantry
        To rubble, the let's-cut-the-bullshit laugh

That now too is ash. O my sister, my Greater
    Maker, your sinewed & capacious sentences
        Unspool through this labyrinth of event

& accident, like Ariadne's thread. Your subjects:
    Love & beauty, which is to say
        Our transience. *For so long, I wanted*

My past back, but now it's the future
    That's burnished with possibility—the tang
        Of saltwater, diagonals of rain. Vases

Of tulips looking out a closed window
    On the snow . . . In a bookstore in 2050
        A girl picks through the poetry shelves:

Their musty smells, the garish fin-de-siècle covers,
    Outdated as handheld cell phones,
        Gasoline cars. & the dead with their compulsion

For oblivion, selves preserved
    As logarithm, data & kitsch.
        But the girl—she loves the feathery heft

Of the thin contraptions, the yellowed paper,
    Weave of quarter cloth bound over board
        & the airy frayed dust jackets,

Their origami flutter in her hands.
    & *Dark Familiar's* caught her eye, signed
        Edition, price reduced to $425

& she haggles with the old man dozing
    At the register, until they settle on $300.
        She'll give up bus fare tonight

& walk, though the rain's giving way
    To big starbursting flakes. Something
        About your poems: the elegant measures,

the fucked-up valedictories of our lives,
　　　Spliced solos with their beauty unbroken:
　　　　　It quickens her heart. Dear shade,

do I have your permission
　　　To say it in that way? *Quicken & Heart,*
　　　　　Pulse & iamb, the blood's retablo & the girl

Lays down her hundreds & walks out to the snow.

　　　—in memoriam, Aleda Shirley

For Tomas Tranströmer

Down Commercial to Land's End, your gait slow,
    rooftop shimmer & the wheeling gulls,
        gable & widow's walk—you're taking it in,

with the almost feral gaze of those
    who store the world under pressure, carbon diamonding.
        The Foc'sle & The Eye of Horus, Town Hall

& the March light intractable, hammered tin
    against the Bay. Beside me half my life ago,
        you amble. My fabulously silly poems had

everything to learn & you'd just made them
    half as long. & now by the town pier we come to it,
        a crowd of half a dozen, circling the dolphin

beached beside an upturned skiff, some waiters
    from the Mayflower dipping checkered
        tablecloths in seawater & laving them

against the putty-colored flanks. Mostly we are silent;
    mostly we stare. Shallow rise & fall of the wet
        ginghamed skin. Someone from the Coast Guard

will be coming too late. Half a life ago.
    & always the future setting forth, beyond where my pen
        can summon this back, beyond where Tomas

can inch his stroke-straightened frame to a bench
    & flex his one good hand above the keyboard ivory, region
        where the faces are shadow, masked & opaque,

crouching to check the drips & monitors, the bed
    repositioned, where the soul floats clumsy
        as a child's balloon to land

on the banks of a place that is not Styx or Lethe,
       but a tourist town off-season. & the soul
              may linger there at last or always. The wind

off Long Point is rising. Tomas bends down,
       his hand stroking beak & forehead, dorsal fin & spine.
              He's taken off his gloves, the leather jacket,

talking low, in Swedish, almost a whisper, his eye
       against the great black pool of eye, twin gazes affixed,
              the way, when two mirrors are set against each other

they fuse to a single burnished infinity.

II.

Another Epistle to Frank O'Hara

—On the Forty-Ninth Birthday of "The Day Lady Died"

It is 3:00 in the torpid New South, three days past Bastille Day & yes
  this is the form you fashioned,
isn't it? Exact & fast & haunted as the opening chords of "Sweet Jane"
  (Mott the Hoople version),
which pulses from the minivan as I drive from shrink to soccer camp, shirtpocket
  staining my new Rx with sweat,

the bank thermometer flashing 103, the day's new record. We still
  use Fahrenheit, Frank
(if I may call you Frank). I might add that we are in deep shit,
  icecaps turning slush,
a gallon of regular more pricey than an opera ticket, not to mention
  a pair of wars, one of which

just killed a reservist—the husband of my son's kindergarten teacher.
  IED, it's called: your body parts
sail for blocks. How do you explain this to a six-year-old, Frank?
  Gauloises & Strega & your endless
namechecks seem beside the point; even the willowy & ravished
  junkie whisper of late

Lady Day cannot console. They have confiscated our cabaret licenses
  & men in camouflage turn men
in orange jumpsuits into whimpering fetal balls. Head slap, stress position,
  waterboard. Explain this
to a six-year-old. Today in the shrink-office *Time*, an obit for
  your long-lived buddy

Robert Rauschenberg—*the trick is not to impose order but to make
  the most of chaos.*
Uh huh. The Odyssey's—yes that's the name, *Odyssey Espresso*—unwieldy
  as a subway car & I'm running

yellow lights to make it on time to the Y, where Jake will stand
        by the potted doorway marigolds,

backpack, NASA baseball cap, his new black soccer cleats
        in hand. Then together
it's hardware store & CVS: ant killer, a/c filters, orange tabs
        to twist the dials of serotonin,
a goofy card for Noelle's fiftieth. Also her grocery list: milk, dinner,
        eggs, cheap pinot noir & a cheaper

(*please*, David) chardonnay this time. My skills at self-portraiture,
        we can both agree,
are limited. At two a.m. most nights I wake in terror. I pray
        to your good spirit, Frank,
that I be worthy of this life, longer than yours already by a decade
        & a half. & I am back

in a Minnesota dorm room, eighteen, snow occluding Fourth Street,
        colder than today by
one hundred degrees, & spellbound I page your big new phonebook-sized
        Collected, the "suppressed"
Larry Rivers cover, where naked you stand, posing Rodin-ishly.
        (Where is it now? Tattered

& worth a dozen tanks of premium.) & it's grace to be born
        & to live as variously as possible.
Grace o soccer cleat, Xanax, Odyssey, grace o standin-on-the-corner
        -suitcase-in-my-hand,
o seasons, o castles, o elegant & gracious & bedazzling Noelle,
        who waiteth for me to uncork

Rex Goliath. Grace o box set *Billie Holiday: The Final Sessions*,
        orchid ashimmer in her lacquered hair.
& Congressional hearings—Rumsfeld, Addington, Yoo: let's start
        the war crimes trial *now*. Grace o milk,
dinner, eggs, o Chamber of the Felines at Lascaux, o my damaged
        life mask of Keats on the wall,

who now, poor bloke, looks trepanned. Grace o Microsoft Word
      (fucked up as it is), Grace
o songs of Junior Parker, Robyn Hitchcock, Grant McLennan. & wise
      George Oppen—
did you know him, Frank?—writing thusly in his *Daybook:*
      you men may wish

to write poetry. At 55, my desires are more specific.

Self-Portrait as Sock Puppet

My son offers eyes, scavenging the plastic box
& gluing me lidless near the hole

beneath my cranium. Now the images pour forth—
table strewn alchemical.
      A button for the nostrils

& he bends to offer breath from dust, a mouth
of pipe cleaner, coiled to enable speech.

Sequin & bead unsilence me, affixed against each temple.
Thus he bids me speak
     & I obey, for he touches

my fledgling tongue with a glowing coal.
Yarn for my hair, yarn for my chin & he teaches

sound by sound the shimmering unhanseled
quaver that becomes my name. I speak

it brokenly, not yet certain what I am.
Fingers curl.
    Into my new skin he guides my hand.

Ode to Black 6

To your veins we've clogged with butter
we give thanks, to your brain tumor withering

the use of your left side, to Alzheimer's
befuddling your stumble through the labyrinth,

indifferent now to females in estrous,
to positive reinforcement, *merci.* For cystic fibrosis,

ALS, mad cow; for rickets, diabetes, dengue
fever, our gratitude. The thirty-five-gauge needles

in the loose fur bristling your neck
have worked their contagion ceaselessly

since 1921. A hundred hundred generations
o my brethren & all your lives

you train, prepare, endure.
The gerrymandered cataracts cannot stall

your progress through the windings
of the maze—Milton flying blind

toward Calvin's God. Push the lever,
eat & retrace your sightless scurry.

Week upon week on the marathon dance floor
we command you to foxtrot & the winning

couple staggers toward their crumb
of cheddar. Death is a Master from

Livermore Lab, the NIH. Your golden fur
Josefina, your ashen fur Stuart Little.

Pipsqueak Terminator from the sequel versions
engineered to save our wayward species,

any cost. You pass through
the refining fires, fur singed,

manic prehensile tail dragging broken.
Push the lever push the lever, nothing

given yet you push & push. Your photo
glowers at me from *National Geographic*.

Upright you stand in the maze's corner,
front paws curled pugilistic,

one of Velazquez's palace dwarfs, leashed
& collared in lace, but staring us down.

No pasaran. Don't tread on me.
Snatch me bastard by the neck & tail

& fuck with me all that you want.
I serve you at my whim.

Mixtape to Be Brought to Her in Rehab

Black lacquered circle & the sound coaxed
    from diamond to rest within the acetate glimmer,
        the agon & the joys commingling. Nina Simone

is conjuring the boat of Ra Little Darling
    from a long cold lonely winter, though outside
        it is August & is not all right. Double doors,

then again double doors. You will sign yourself in:
    & they'll rifle through your bag of oranges & candy bars,
        pry open the plastic case & hold the gray

Maxell against the light. Immense are the tears
    of Levi Stubbs. How sweet how sweet the honeybee.
        The Smiths are in a terrible place. O Oscillate

Wildly Please Please Please Let Me Get What I Want,
    to be followed in turn by Mr. James Brown,
        his own pleas trembling the Apollo rafters.

Visiting hours—in the TV room the Haldol reigns.
    Reagan struts among the SS gravestones,
        pompadour shiny as a new LP, his movie-actor gait

turned thank God to pastel vapor by *Miami Vice.*
    Flamingos starburst from the credits. Shyly
        she will walk the corridor to meet you, your offerings

of Earl Grey, the two black turtlenecks.
    Nails cobalt—fingers a-tremble. Gun-Shy, Screaming
        Blue Messiahs, Dylan at his nadir adenoiding

Brownsville Girl—*even the swap meets around here*
    are getting a little corr-rupt. Richard Thompson
        When the Spell Is Broken, Jimmy Cliff's

in limbo waiting for the dice to roll.
      When her roommate leaves, you'll sit with her upon the bed.
        Awkward you will small-talk, staring

at your hands. More doors, double doors & triple,
      the years the years. Down the carved names
        the future with its labyrinths & tailspins, rooms

giving way to rooms, the upturned car, the notebooks
      cuneiformed with numbers, pivot & gyre, cache
        of Rx pads stuffed into a rolltop drawer. ninety rabid

troubled minutes, coda Robert Johnson. Stones in my
      passway & my road seem dark as night. Her eyes in memory
        an astonished blue. You reach inside your jacket

& she holds it in her upturned palm. From the bedside
      table she lifts the Walkman—the button with its triangle,
        the click, the whir, the eddying forward.

Jimmie Rodgers's Last Blue Yodel, 1933

There were twelve of them before it, & they made him

something grander than a yodeling brakeman: "a star of screen & stage"

etc., but a minor one & broke, with a ticket to a final hemorrhage

in NYC, Victor Studios. He yodels as the crimson phlegm

lavas out to ruin his Sunday suit. They've got him propped

with pillows on a cot, & he's singing that he's free

o he's free from the chain gang now, his follow-up to "TB

Blues," his last real hit, itself the follow-up to "Whippin'

That Old TB." He needs to make enough from tunes

to pay for a proper sanitarium: the hillbilly Keats

of my father's 78s, red-yodeling his blues,

his Negative Capability Rag, into an antique

microphone, his name writ on railroad ties. Two days later

he was on his way to Mississippi in a box.

For Willy DeVille

—1950–2009

To your tatts that sprawled like continents, the cloud-compounded planet—
cadmium, ultramarine—spied from 17,000 miles afar,
to the sax yelping likewise High Celestial, the chords & strings

& choruses you lifted from Spector, Piaf, Muddy, The Wolf
& Ben E. King, piano riffs Latino morphing Crescent City, influence
alchemized to dire conviction. & you with that *voice*—

volume lurching croon to baritone to snarl, coyote howl
& aye-yah-yah & home most frequently your left inner arm,
dappled red. & now you've at last outlived yourself,

reduced to your dwindled cultic fans, to Big in Europe
& to my speakers on a winter morning, where your harp
caterwauls madly to "Just Your Friends," the castanets & strings

conspiring to a mini-epic of obsessive love.
Fucked-up, fucked-up like us, though your gift survives us all.
Earth, receive your honored guest. *Le Chat Bleu*

is laid to rest. Dazzling Stranger, let the saxes keen
their long Big Easy funeral. *This must be the niiiggghhht*
I can feel it to my FINger-tips. Maybe just around the CORner

someone's waitin' for me . . . You gave us more
than we deserved, which is one means to factor
the radiant necessity of art, a pale cadaverous junkie

strumming a battered Martin just redeemed from pawn.
You give me a night a quarter-century forgotten, some club
in Kentish Town or Camden where you wail

'til morning—first to still the din of clinking pints,
the Woodbine fog, then to inhabit the soul's bitter essence—
a voice so pleading that the room was shamanized.

Christopher was there & Lynda alive & black-bereted.
You ate of our sins; you spit them out in a style of prayer.
Second encore: "Heaven Stood Still." You've peeled off

the black silk shirt, mike stand in your fingers but you're
on your knees, the proper stance for a ballad so yearning,
the whispered lyrics & your gold tooth shining forth.

The proper stance, Willy: your grave & supplicant moan unending.

The Apotheosis of Charlie Feathers

> Then the Shadow perceived there was a stronger one than It.
> —NAG HAMMADI LIBRARY

Elision & a battered Gibson, high-hat sizzle & the anviling thump of slapback.
        The object:
communicate the traceries of such pain, moan & glottal hiccup, the blunder
        of the soul betrayed,
bark & rasp, the sullen chords of "I Can't Hardly Stand It" (*King 4971*,
        7/56). *Well the sun's*

gone down & you're uptown . . . & thus Charlie Feathers is lifted up,
        his ascension
wreathed in feedback. By the truculent conch of the throat we are summoned.
        The jealous heart
unfolds its cobra hood, bob & weave, the tongue flicking madly & the venom
        spit, *you troublin' me.*

The hurt parts the waters. *You got me all tore up, all tore up.* Bodily
        Charlie Feathers ascends.
Stardom has eluded him & he ascends. Reading neither music nor the alphabet,
        he ascends. Cheated by fate,
Sun Records & Elvis Presley, his singles warped in basement trunks,
        thrift shop & landfill, he ascends.

Ars longa & we know the rest. I push *repeat* & again he wails. I-95's
        backed up for miles,
my windshield filigreed with sleet. I'm turning off the engine as an ambulance
        lurches up the shoulder
pulsing red. Home is close & hours away. A busted umbrella,
        beneath which a woman stands

& fidgets, smoking on a median laced with broken glass & fast-food bags.
        Of matter corrupt,
deluded gods did fashion the material world, America its purest product.
        A roadside at sundown,

the wet ditch aglitter with points of light. Thrice-Great Charlie Feathers
        did not read the Gnostics,

but from America he concocted his means of transport. Teleology of wail.
        Fuck these puny gods.
Archon, demiurge: you touch not e'en his garment's hem. From West Helena,
        he ascends. From the green-
glowing dials of Depression Philcos, he ascends. I push *repeat.*
        & I'm still he-re,

a-sittin' round, all tore up, got me all tore up. . . . Ahead, a semi's brakelights
        flicker on. Along the far shoulder,
the ambulance returns, cigarette to the pavement, umbrella jimmied shut.
        Forward through affliction, through
the garbled light we inch; we gather speed. Home is closer. I twist the dial,
        volume to ten. Watch out, ye Archons,

Charlie Feathers is tuning up.

World Tree

> ... it is considered best to choose a tree that has been struck by lightning.
> —MIRCEA ELIADE, *SHAMANISM*

FORMAT I: 78
—*1957*

Hank Williams is thick shellac. Hank Williams
is so lonesome he could cry. & in the basement my father stands,

the black grooves' slick pomade atremble in his hands.
Lonesome whippoorwill.
                    The saber saw hums

& stutters off. He needles the lonesome again.
Weary weary blues from waiting. This the procedure,

this the rite. At the doorway I hover
unseen, awl & woodscrew. My Zorro cape's an apron.

Tick, tick tick when the needle closes circle,
goodbye Joe.
                    Copper glint of bourbon bottle

two-thirds gone, shoved back to where it's hidden on the shelf
behind the woodstain & the turpentine. Needle closes circle,

tick, tick. Bladewail, sawdust. Lost Highway,
take these chains.
                    Startled, he turns to me.

FORMAT II: 8-TRACK & SELECTRIC
—*1977*

Startled, she turns from a reverie
two parts gin, one part *The Soundtrack to Dr. Zhivago,*

its recipe unvarying. Turns to me
as ice cubes rattle & the balalaikas swell.

My mother jams the squat red cartridge in the stereo—
violin murk over tape hiss,
                              the tinny sleigh bells

conspiring to
                 a confessional poem. My IBM Selectric
awaits like a phaeton, Courier 10-point

incising its mirrorball, elegant serifs
that are never my life,
                              nor hers. A swig

or two more & she's out. The ice cubes
melt, for it's spring in the Urals.
                                      The sleigh is mud-locked

but the poem goes on, & the ball will rotate
to its melody of brittle grief, black acetate.

FORMAT III: 45
    —1964

"Don't Worry, Baby"'s falsetto of grief: the sleek black wax
coaxed from its sleeve, where the Beach Boys in identical stripes

are all grin & tan. But dread lurks
in the high notes & the bass line. The race

is tomorrow. The narrative is pure *High Noon*.
"I can't back down now . . ."
                              Panic in the voice

of Brian Wilson, who has "pushed the other guy too far." Soon
it all will change. The surfboard of innocence

will wipe out & drown. Dead cosmonauts will wheel in space.
The other guy
                will lose both legs in Laos.

But now Brian's girl shall look him in the face,
commending him not to fear.
                        The Jag gleams & purrs.

My mind's eye turns it Cinemascope, color resolution
Alamogordo bright.
                I set the needle down again.

FORMAT IV: FIELD RECORDING
    —1937

The drum is sinew, feather & reindeer skin,
fashioned from tree struck by lightning.

Static from a microphone, the cylinder is creaking.
Drumbeat. Argu Banyut moaning.
                        He ascends

The World Tree, eyes aflutter, a realm where Dr. Markov
cannot follow. The yurt is gray with smoke.

Rung by rung & branch by branch. The dead speak
birdsong, wolf-howl. Drumbeat.
                        He arrives

at their camp. They are phantom shape & animal soul,
adrift in the Other World's
                        boundless forests.
Drumbeat. 6,000 versts to the west,
gulag labor gouges out
                        the White Sea Canal.

Decrees are signed—the latest purge. Drumbeat,
birdsong, wolf-howl. The dead & their guttering speech.

FORMAT V: 33⅓

—*1965*

Alamogordo bright—I set the needle down again
on "Desolation Row." Postcards of the hanging

as the marchers pour across the Pettus Bridge—
then the clubs, the dogs unleashed,
                                    the fire hoses seething

at the center of a low dishonest decade
where selves grow immense, then shrink

to pinpoint size, flickering like fireflies.
O the ghost of electricity
                        howls ectoplasmic

in the bones of all our faces. Dylan
stands frail with his Strat at Newport

Gotterdammerung loud on "Maggie's Farm."
Tear-gassed King retreats to Selma. Cronkite

in a flight suit narrates bombs above Hanoi.
Lord Self sets the bitter diamond down again.

FORMAT VI: CASSETTE

—*1994*

Pearling from me, the sticky bitter salt.
Her tongue & my sudden groan. This

swallowed too, for we hadn't touched in months.
Pewter morning,
                    the first snow of her last year hissing soft.

I am called upon to reconstruct the room,
though it was almost bare. Marianne Faithfull,

nicotine-ravaged, unspooling "Sister Morphine,"
"Strange Weather"
                              from a battered boombox. I am called upon

to watch her rise & scurry to the dresser,
flipping the tape in the room's sudden chill

& all over the world—the precise guttural
moan—*strangers*
                    talk only 'bout the weather.

I am called upon to summon up her face, her hand
against her mouth,
                    & the tape & the snow circle on.

FORMAT VIII: CD
   —2004

& thus the dead convene: the voices swirl on,
missives from the afterlife,
                              laser-guided like a bomb,

chronicling this Exodus, this dreadlocked dream,
of end time & deliverance. Marley's "Redemption

Song," given voice by the gravel majesty
of dead Johnny Cash,
                          dueting with the dead

Joe Strummer, trading verses, shaky harmony
at the chorus, the unchained paradise of Garvey.

O won't you help me sing—Cash with his Lion
of Judah growl—
                    these songs of freedom. Strummer

a beat behind, but lo the voices entwine.
The righteous shall prevail. The Downpresser

topple & break like a reed. The dead arisen.
Our offering: these plates of silver in our hands.

FORMAT VIII: DOWNLOAD, SHAMANIC

Let go the dead, somber from their backdrops
    of extravagant azaleas. Let go
        their faces from the Spirit World,

sepia their corporal's stripes, black & white
    their scarved profiles, posing gravely,
        vamping for their jacket photos.

Let go the dead, return. Morning in summer,
    Noelle asleep at last, up half the night
        with our sons until the fevers broke.

Let go the dead. Upstairs the boys
    are waking, murmuring in their beds
        to one another from the dreams

of four-year-olds, cartoon balloon
    & sound collage, monsters sprouting
        multiple eyes, yet no more fearsome

than the shouted stammer
    of Joey Ramone, the *gabba gabba hey*
        the boys love to pogo to in their playroom.

Fast song again please, fast song again.
    Their feet stomp above me. Let go the dead,
        return. Invoke the spirit helpers

in the Secret Language, for the journey back
    is perilous. Summon the raven. Summon
        the owl. Drumbeat pulsing the Spirit World

where all speech arrives as song.
        Language remade. Language prolonged.
            The spirit helpers leave their perches.

By the skin drum they are summoned.
        Let go the dead, return
            through the pathways & the airwaves,

sing the rungs of the World Tree,
        song of three chords, song of abreaction.
            The dead are countenanced, let go.

The dead arisen. From the cul de sacs
        of neural mazes, return, from wax
            & acetate, from the white diamond light

lasering words to our ears, return.
        Verse chorus verse. 7 a.m.,
            the second of June. Above me

the boys dance circles until
        the ceiling trembles. *Gabba gabba*
          hey. Fast song again please.

Return, return. It is here that I
        shall dwell. The morning blazes up
            & my speech shall not be confounded.

III.

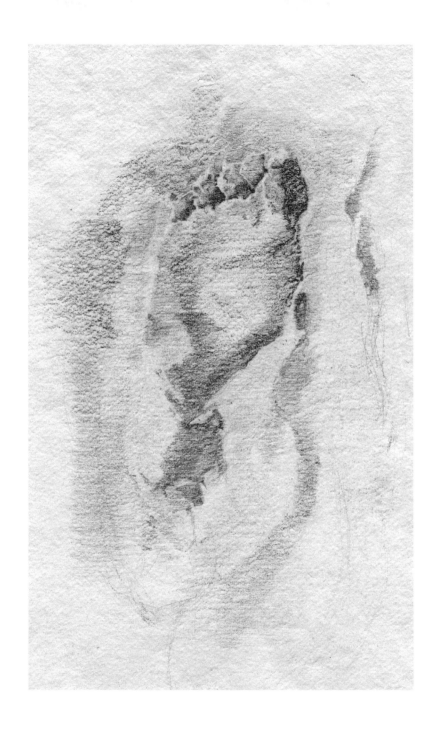

Ochre

i.

FOOTPRINT & TORCH WIPE

(*Chauvet, c. 27,000 BP*)

Something of us to prove our afterlife.
Hurried with charcoal on the cave wall of Chauvet.

The hands drip ochre; they fumble with the Kodak.
What is your mother's maiden name, your wife's

Middle initial? Favorite sport or pet? You have successfully
Changed your password.
                              The footprints of the cave's

Last visitor tell us he was ten or twelve.
We know his height—approx. 4' 3".

As his pine-pitch torch tapered down, he'd wipe
The ashen top against the cave side, once against an auroch,

Once against a cave bear, the way my father would flick
The wavering orange tip of his Lucky Strike

From his lawn chair to the fireflied grass. Our leavings.
The boy crawled lightward,
                              on his feet the pollen of an Aurignacian spring.

ii.

**THIS IS OUR BOY, DOG AND CAT AND I AM STICKING MY
NOSE THROUGH THE BACK OF THE CHAIR. BURNS JUST
WOKE UP SO HE LOOKS KIND OF MUSSED UP**

(Gelatin, Silver Print, c. 1910)

They have scurried to their moment, this botched alignment
Of the stars & planets. Mother is eye through slat,

Half-mask, shard of mouth, an Indiana Cubist.
The Lab, the calico, Burns unsteady on the chair back.

She props them all, a juggler stasised on a unicycle,
Dress spilling over chair legs, the Oriental's

Snaking figurations & rosettes—both parallel
& askew, depth uncertain, the formal

"studio effect" that Mother planned
Disheveled as Burns' spiky pudding bowl.

Salome the cat's a feline blur, head pendulumed
& poised to spring back to the feral present

Mother labored mightily to still.
A handprint framed in ochre, quickened on a cave wall.

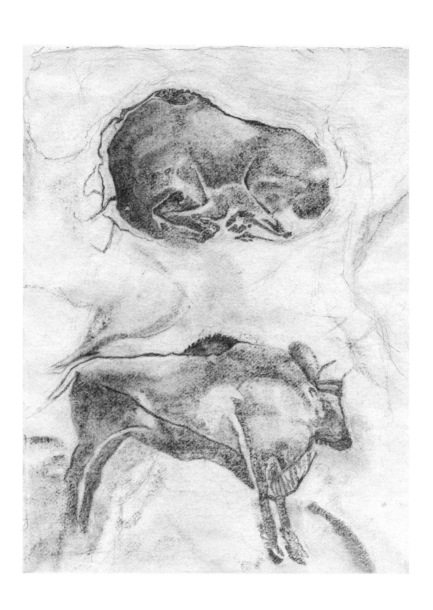

iii.

HALTED BISON BELLOWING, RECLINING BISON TURNING ITS HEAD

(Altamira, c. 17,600 BP)

We are designed for the moment, writes late
& dying Lowell. Down the Serengeti trees

Bipedal we descended to savannah grass:
Taking notice, all eye & larynx.
                                        We lie in wait

& make the kill—a newborn gazelle,
Sliced from its skin with an artless handaxe—

Taking notice of the Alpha Male's technique.
Now step forward a thousand thousand generations, until

The ice pulls back from the cliffs of the Dordogne
& a pair of covert eyes records the bison herd

So minutely, each face & tuft of hair, each twist of neck
Is hoarded into memory.
                                 Against the limestone

Synapse guides hand, pulsing to release the crimson forms,
Stilled as they bellow, stilled as—to us—they turn.

iv.

SOME OF THE GOOFS AT CAMP *PHANTOM WOOD*
"We Will Make a Good Beginning"
K. Hoff

> (Gelatin Silver Plate, c. 1910)

Furthermore, the moment may be festooned:
The moment's upgrade, its bonus track,

Moment embellished, an alternate take—
By Jimmy By Cracker Hot Dog 23 Skidoo.

The Five Goofs, wreathed in lakewater up to their chests,
Have been Photoshopped
                              by the expert

Fountain penstrokes of K. Hoff, artist
& ringmistress. To each face she's administered a *mask*,

Rictusing to all a grin or laugh, eyebrows
& 'staches absurdly hirsute a la Groucho

Or Agamemnon sneering from his grave mask, hammered gold.
The sky has been improved by two smudged birds.

Caption: *Amos Smelser has been marked as "A." The "G"*
Is H. Goodwin.
                    Having Good Fun, aren't we?

V.

THE ALCOVE OF THE LIONS

    (Chauvet, c. 32,000 BP)

Furthermore, the moment may be emblazoned
To honor mysteries
                beyond plot or intention.

The horses thunder past two roaring lions.
The artist, we know, sketched quickly & blended

All four figures to a blurred kinetic fusion.
Both inside & outside the bellies of the lions,

The horses may already be prey.
                    Or like two fast freights
Horse & lion rattle down their parallel tracks

Each to its own insistent destination. Nothing random,
Yet nothing to assuage our questions or our longing—

Which is one definition of myth. Deliver us from our abjection
O Lords of Spirit Realm & Hunting Magic.

We are but charcoal, ink & pixel before Thy
Manifold unspeakability.
                  May our hands be nimble & steady.

Fig 1.
The Photograph by Mrs Deane
(Faces of sitters obliterated)

vi.

COLONEL ALLERTON S. CUSHMAN, HIS WIFE AND THE
SPIRIT OF ANNABELLE, THEIR DECEASED DAUGHTER,
WITH THE SITTERS' FACES BLOTTED OUT TO PROTECT
THEIR IDENTITIES

*Ada Emma Deane, Photographer: Journal of the American Society
for Psychic Research 16*

(*Gelatin Silver Plate, 1922*)

& when does moment transfigure to myth?
& who drives its tableaus & trapdoors, the cables

Enabling flight? The credulous & gullible—
Shamanized or conned?
                                    The dearly departed is froth

& smudge. She hovers ectoplasmically
Above her mother's hat, mother whose own face

Has been scoured to iconoclastic nothingness.
Back ramrod straight, the colonel squats uneasily,

Visage tabula rasa, awaiting from The Other Side
Some signal, token, evidence. Annabelle's

Dear Voice, or her Spirit Writing, ethereal
In the turbid studio dark; a lock of hair to materialize

& for an instant, hold. *We are poor passing facts,*
Named but faceless.
                                    Each of us a famished ghost.

vii.

SIXTY-FIVE STENCILED HANDS, FORTY-FOUR IN BLACK AT
THE FURTHEREST REACHES OF THE CAVE AND TWENTY-ONE
STENCILED IN RED ON A WALL CLOSER TO THE ENTRANCE.
THE MOST COMMON POSITION FOR MUTILATED HANDS IS
WITH RING AND LITTLE FINGER HELD DOWN

(Cosquer, c. 27,000 BP)

First, go forth & find a reed through which to pour yourself.
Inhale, exhale. For days you have danced & chanted,

Drinking only your own blood from a chalice
Spiked with belladonna, mushroom,
                              your clansmen's spit.

Now ready your palette. The cheeks balloon. Exhale
& the mixture wreathes each finger. Your mouth & lips

Are red as hemorrhage. Down your chin it trails.
The taste of ochre surges & ebbs

Or the bitter synesthetic tang of charcoal
Darkens both mouth & torchlit wall.
                              Our selves'

Relentless shuttle—we are form & function, solo
& clan. The oldest of the women hefts

A child toward the ceiling. He bends two fingers down.
From his lips
            the self flares out incarnadine.

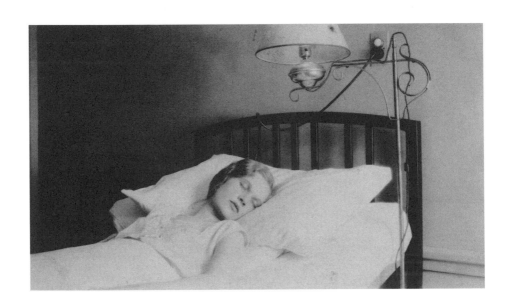

viii.

THIS IS THE ONE WHEN I WAS ASLEEP. I HAD BEEN IN THE
HOSPITAL ALMOST A MONTH SO I LOOK KIND OF WORN
DOWN. THE PICTURE DOES NOT DO MY ROOM JUSTICE. IT
WAS ALL IN PINK AND BLUE. I HAD A FRENCH TELEPHONE
BESIDE MY BED ON THE RADIO THAT DOESN'T SHOW UP
HERE. REALLY IT WAS WONDERFUL HOW THE HOSPITAL
ROOMS ARE SO CHEERFUL AND SO MUCH LIKE A HOTEL
ROOM

    (Gelatin Silver Plate, c. 1930)

This, dear Ida, was my first full night of sleep
Since arriving in Santa Fe. Maria the nurse,

Who I've grown quite fond of (though she speaks
little English), has a Kodak of her own.
                      The flash

Didn't wake me. I could have slumbered through Judgment Day.
The evening before—do not be alarmed, my dear—

I coughed two cups of blood into a basin
While Maria propped up my head.
                      But then the night terror

Vanished. The sunset turned the light a dusty saffron.
& let me tell you a curious dream: Dr. Weiss

Had wheeled me to a vaulted room. We both had *lab coats* on.
Under his microscope he lodged the slide. "This

Kingdom lies within," he whispered—the good tissue muddy brown,
The bacilli a stunning blue
                & swift as minnows they swam.

ix.

THE KILLED MAN

(Cougnac, c. 15,000 BP)

The stick man bristles with five sticks
& his insides pour out, a mesh of ochre,

Rendered childlike. The invention of torture
Is so fresh they are confounded.
                                    How to depict

The human figure mangled, the whole reduced
To the gutted sum of its parts, a brilliant ooze

Of sinew? Some long-forgotten deity is appeased
Or praised.
                    It eats & eats of our flesh.

They keep you chained & hooded on the flight
From Kabul to Gitmo. They serve a meal

Of rubber hoses, then another. The shackles
Gnaw at your wrists & ankles. Then it's straight

From tarmac to solitary. They tug off the cowl. The light
Strikes you down.
                        On fettered hands & knees, crawl.

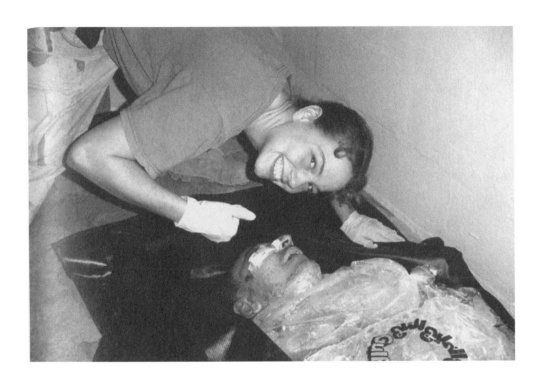

X.

**SABRINA HERMAN, SOLDIER IN THE 372ND MILITARY
POLICE COMPANY, POSES IN FRONT OF THE BODY OF
MANADEL AL-JAMADI AT ABU GHRAIB PRISON**

(Digital, 2004)

Unzip the body bag; then rustle through
A second layer of heavy plastic. Pull

It down to unwrap the face: a Russian doll
With duct-taped eyes,

      mouth a puckered *o*,

Hawk nose, shaved head paisleyed with contusion.
Twist it slightly for a better angle.

Now we're talking Smile Sabrina Smile.
& the latex glove, hovering thumbs up—the punctum

Arranging everything, like Mousterian tools
In a test trench.
     Shanidar Cave: a Neanderthal male,

Half-blind with a withered arm, impossibly old
At forty, receives his grave-goods—armloads

Of burdock, cornflower, hollyhock.
       & a cache of flints
For the perilous & beflowered afterlife.

xi.

SKELETON OF A MAMMOTH, EMBEDDED WITH EIGHT CLOVIS SPEARPOINTS

(Naco, NM, c. 10,800 BP)

Comely & most fair are their shapes. How they glow
Bloodflecked in dawnlight, svelte & pulchritudinous.

Resplendent the flaking, the hafting, the binding with sinew,
Worked for hours, worked for days,
        tooled upon the mind's

Impeccable lathe, tooled to in a second razor
Through hide & muscle, to heat-seek the heart,

The huge baggy lungs brimming over
With blood,
    sharp-flecked punctum, the thesis statement

Written through the eye, embedded in the frontal lobe.
So the prey stumbles down, the lungs

Still laboring, the haunches flensed. We stab
& climb the flanks, the real work beginning. I am become

Death, the shatterer of worlds, tooled & supernoval.
We clean our spearpoints—
       foaming red the serpentine arroyo.

xii.

LOS ALAMOS: OPPENHEIMER'S SON PETER, WITH HIS FATHER'S PIPE

(Gelatin Silver Plate, 1944)

Endless days of nannies with security clearance:
Marta with her face mole, a trio of long white hairs

Feathering from its center. She hums to Glenn Miller.
She does not slap him as Carmela did.
                                        English

Is not her strong suit. Endless days he watches
The clock edge to 3 above the woodstove,

Chalk dust shimmering the air. Cursive, cursive,
Cursive. Uppercase & lower.
                              One-room schoolhouse

& outside Jeeps grind gears in quagmire streets.
Trucks lug heavy water to the detonation site.

My   nameis   Peter   Thetownwhere I live   does   not exist.

MY NAME   IS PETER MY TOWN DOES NOT EXIST.

*Some nights I wake to father hoem he's a book a drink
A radioh*
            This is me and his pipe   It tastes jst like a cough

xiii.

SEVERAL RELIEFS DEPICTING VULTURES

(Gobekli Tepe, c. 12,000 BP)

> Some cultures have long believed that high flying carrion birds
> transported the flesh of the dead up to heaven . . .

World door, crimson your geometry.
Our flesh ascends the heaven-road. The air now thins.

Red-hooded Charon pilots us in spirals, laboring
Up to the precincts
     where stars commence.

As words that are unspoken, he bears us in his mouth.
Entrails & viscera, we are the salt tang

Of sinew, of marrow, of the word made flesh.
A jigsaw of syllables to be arranged

Once more to human form. The sky gods await us there.
In vast huts & tents
     they ready their tools.

Brother vulture spits us out upon the tent floor.
We writhe & quicken to verb & glottal.

Eye socket, nostril: they mold the clay. They bestow
The mouth from which we words shall burrow.

xiv.

VICE PRESIDENT RICHARD CHENEY DONNING A GAS MASK: IMAGE SUPPRESSED FOR SECURITY REASONS

(Digital, 2002)

> On the backseat behind him rested a duffel bag stocked with a gas mask and a biochemical survival suit.
> —JANE MAYER, *THE DARK SIDE*

I am ready for my close-up, Mr. DeMille.
The devolution
                is almost complete.

I am three hundred eyes, I ingest
Mine enemies. I *smite* them. I am Kali.

Arms every which way. I need no hazmat
In my new post-human form.
                      The enhanced

Interrogation commences: I gobble your head.
I am programmed to swallow your thoughts.

They pulse within me. We shall know each other now.
I turn you to sugar in my thorax.

I know your confederates. I mantis your networks.
My location is secure. They stop the limo

So that I may digest you better. The motorcade
Halts & hums.
                When will you know you have died?

XV.

TREPANNED SKULL OF A WOMAN WITH A PROSTHETIC
SEASHELL EAR

(Roque d'Aille, c. 6,000 BP)

The facts: someone made a drill of flint
& bore into her cranium for hours,

                                    a procedure

She survived, living on some twenty years.
Someone fashioned a device with which she might detect

The wave-crash of a sea three hundred miles away,
Worked shell to a phosphorescent simulacrum

Of auricle & cartilage, a lobe she'd worry
Until her fingers rubbed it smooth as skin.

Of untold mysteries we are composed. Gray matter,
Soul, ether. The light staggered out from the depths,

From synapse, memory, REM state.
                                    & was affliction cured?
& did she prophesize—oracle, priestess, sphinx?

Wounded goddess, did she unclasp her shell-ear as she lay down to dream?
The words are rebus.
                    All we can hear is the guttural sea.

Fig. 67 —P 509 Alexander target

xvi.

THOUGHTOGRAPHY, TED SERIOS: A PART OF A SERIES
PRODUCED BY SERIOS IN THE LABORATORY OF THE
PHYSICIAN JAMES B. HURRY, WHO SUPERVISED THE
PROCEEDINGS. SERIOS WAS PLACED IN AN ELECTRICALLY
INSULATED ROOM CALLED A FARADAY CAGE. HE HAD NO
CONTACT WITH HIS POLAROID CAMERA, HELD IN TURNS
BY EISENBUD & HURRY OUTSIDE THE ROOM

(*Polaroid, 1967*)

The Polaroid accordions open in the doctor's hands.
His labcoat gleams. Within the dark of the Faraday Cage,

Serios sits & sways, seriously stoned
On a hipflask lunch of Crow.
                              Gone are the shakes

& he's free to concentrate. The next room over,
Doctor Hurry in repose before an empty wall—

He clicks the camera toggle down, a whir
As the photo spits out.
                              A month of trials

Leading to a thousand photographs of "mental labor"—
An aerial view of the Denver Hilton, a pillbox

Hat a la Jackie, an iron, a toaster, a blue Corvair,
A Kit Kat bar. Ekphrasis so prosaic

It can't be faked. The Shaman Self spit out to the air
Of the Mile High City.
                              On extended boozy wings, it hovers.

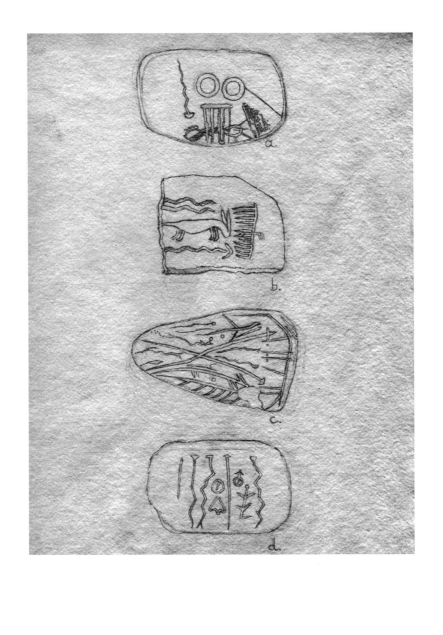

xvii.

FOUR ENGRAVED & GROOVED STONES, POSSIBLY CALENDRICAL

(Jerf el Ahmar, c. 9,300 BP)

Corporeal is our script, we dead
Whose codexes confound you. A slash

To phase the moon, a slash to drive an ibex
Up a self-same alpine stone.
                          Microed

& macroed. Snakehead or sperm? Moon or ovum?
The quick brown fox jumps over the lazy dog,

Password Protected. Strings of a lyre the dead can strum
In glossolalic silence.
                     Incise the slag,

Cut deeper & the gods spew out, commingling
With fist & stylus, stone to stone in its season—

<u>spring</u>   <u>summer</u>   <u>autumn</u>   <u>winter</u>   <u>spring</u>
  3   3   3   3   3

Marrow to marrow, groove & puncture, we factor time:

Red letter dates—all rebus & cipher. The detail work's
Promethean.
            We cleave the graven firmament.

xviii.
QUIXO[T]IC: 248 PTS!!! (TWO TRIPLES & A BINGO)
(Polaroid, 1972)

Q_{10} ueenly, she half-smiles. I pose her

U_1 nder the patio umbrella, sweltering August.

I_1 mperious, she gestures toward the rubied letters,

X_8 s & Os aimed at her son—air kisses to embarrass

O_1 r needle me. She *pushes my buttons,*

T_1 ipsy with her third gin & tonic.

I_1 n the photo, her hair could be her own.

C_2 hemo, though, has shaved her eyebrows clean. **QUIXOTIC—**

A_1 windmill before her, armed with L&Ms & Beefeater's,

B_3 ravely she charges. *Two Hundred Forty-Eight!!*

I_1 n a reverie now, she's thoroughly snockered:

N_1 *ow try to top this, college brat!*

G_3 arrulous, voice still hoarse from the radiation,

O_1 ut of the bag she draws her new letters. A hiss & a grin.

xix.

IN THE CACTUS GALLERY, THE SUPPOSED POSITION
OF THE ARTIST DRAWING A LITTLE RED BEAR, 4 M
(OVER 13 FT) UP ON THE RIGHT WALL

(*Chauvet, c. 31,000 BP*)

This is the steep, uncanny Sistine. Up the wet rock face
You inch. The torch pitches shadows

& lambent you balance on the thinnest of toeholds,
Body splayed,
                    a huge precarious *h*.

The nails of your left hand rake the calcite,
Leaving the right to summon the bear—

Muzzle, hanging lower lip, the ears'
Red disks, blotched like lipstick traces.

You sway; your tendons twist & ache.
You add two curled hairs beneath the jaw.

The spirit realm quickens as you draw
The she-bear
                    wakening to your scent. She shakes

Her vast head, snarls & meets your eyes.
Hold your tranced hand steady
                                        & return her gaze.

XX.

**FROM A TRIPTYCH WHEREIN THE AUTHOR SLAYS
HIS FATHER. NOTE THE FATHER'S SHADOW IN THE
CENTRAL PANEL**

(Chromogenic Print, 1959)

He is gall & shadowplay, a viewfinder
Whose eye is spyglassed, orbing

Some radiance around his son, cantilevered:
The two souls
                weighed upon the balance, throbbing

With the brinkmanship Cold War light. Boy in a gold plastic
Fencing mask, two plastic foils, rubber-tipped

To blunt such struggle. But the story's governed & fixed—
Meet the stranger at the crossroads. Strike

Him down & finish him. He drops to the lawn;
His lids flutter shut
                & when he re-quickens

His shadow joins him once again, horn-rims
Adjusted, a Kool straight lit in a trembling hand

To celebrate his resurrection. Touch the wounds,
He says—the side, the hands.
                      Touch now, it is permitted.

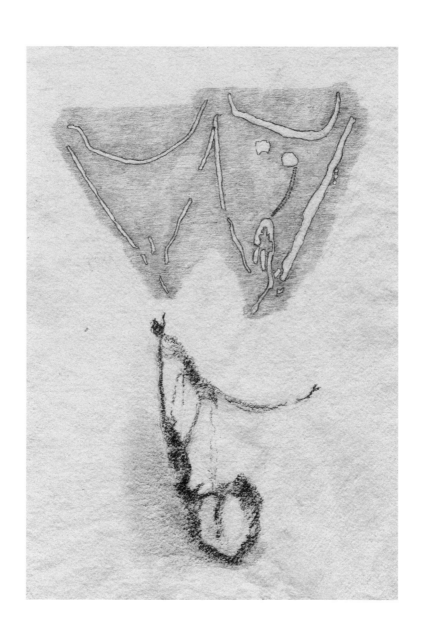

xxi.

FIFTY-FOUR ENGRAVINGS OF PUBIC TRIANGLES

(Lascaux, c. 18,000 BP)

World door, crimson your geometry.
Our flesh descends the birth-river.

We spatter the pubic thistle field copiously—
The shared blood.
                    The quickened pupil of the door

Creaks open to the shrill of light. The doeskin
On the cave floor viscid, matted in the torches'

Orb & spill. Our hands grope, stunned
By this confounding plentitude.
                                   They reach

For the nipple's new moon. A hand axe
Severs our path to the firmaments of water,

The birth cord flung onto the snow. The new moon waxes
With a droplet of alabaster.

We are thrust before it. The mouth has learned to wail,
To fasten, to conjoin. We swallow & we still.

xxii.

THIS ONE DAVEY TOOK FROM THE MIDDLE OF THE BEDROOM WHILE JOHNNY AND I WERE BOTH ASLEEP

(Polaroid Study of the Author's Parents, 1964)

Rafted & tangled in their separate sheets,
Their single-bed dreams depression-poor,

Eyelids aflutter, they snore & fidget,
A watch & earrings
                        their sole commingling, the dresser

Jewelboxed & decanted with their smells.
Insensible persistence,
                        the burning leaves, their pungency.

The world's a book of shadows. The boy stands
Swaying in their bedroom's center, equidistant

Between each cloven city, battlements yet untoppled.
The camera spits out its blur. Bakelite

Transistor from a far room: static & box scores, early Beatles,
October sleet.
                        Neutron, proton, electron, our orbits

Linked & isolate. & one to bear this caption
Graying to another century, block letters in a trembling hand.

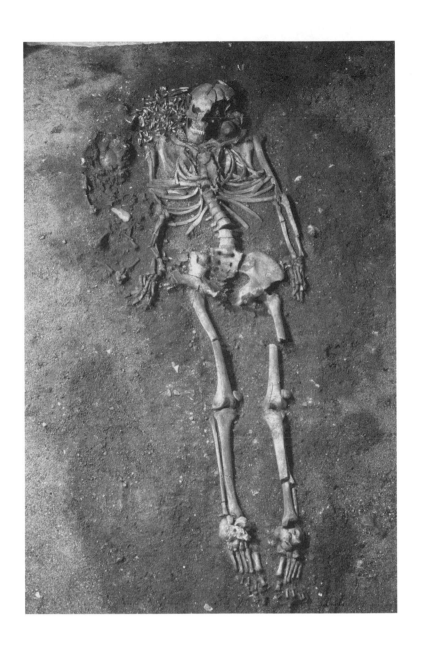

xxiii.

BURIAL OF A YOUNG WOMAN WITH A NEWBORN BABY
BESIDE HER ON A SWAN'S WING

(Vedback, Denmark, c. 6,800 BP)

My tunic—a painted chainmail of snails' shells,
Hundreds, its beadwork my shroud & raiment.

Into the clay I'm lowered. Incantation & spell.
My brothers, sisters, parents.
                    The eyelids—

Open forever, to meet the afterlife awakened.
Crimson ochre hissed through hollow reeds

Covers my face; my eyes dazzle, I died young—
sixteen, eighteen, ochre too rains down upon my pelvis,

Signifying death in childbirth. Beside the shoulders
My stillborn is placed,
               a boy, & he's gripping

an antler spearpoint longer than his torso.
The afterlife, the afterlife.
                  He's cradled on a swan's wing:

The gods' white messenger, the feathered & disjointed pinion,
Which can't be my wing since it is only one.

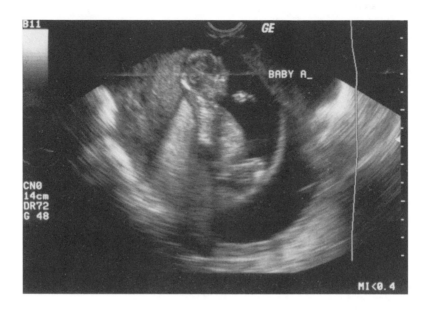

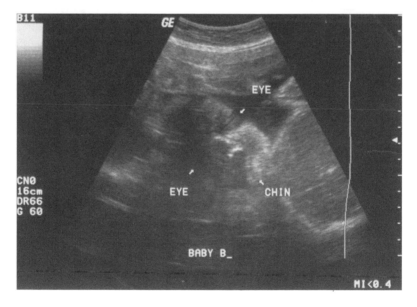

xxiv

SONOGRAM IMAGE OF TWINS

(*Sept. 12, 2001*)

Binary stars, heartbeats dueting—martial
& celestial is the music of the spheres.

Pumped from Andromeda, filtered through gel,
Unspeakably searing,
                              the white-hot craniums, fingers

To clench & unclench, amniotic brine
Of space dust & pneuma, of blastocysts alchemical

& nodding to the office Muzak: Coltrane,
Clifford Brown, *Sketches of Spain* & *Birth of the Cool*

& N's belly paunching in its role as Venus
Of Willendorf. The camera abracadabras,

Rubbing its crystal ball—
                              penis & toe, umbilicus & umbilicus
Gerrymandering their Route 66, twin boats of Ra

Catching some zeds in the amniotic night-towns
Before they burst forth wailing, sails unfurled with dawn.

XXV.

MILITARY PORTRAIT OF MY FATHER

(Kodak, 1944)

—after Rilke

My eyes don't dream, though surely my brow feels
Something remote. Shut lips.
                              Can you penetrate

This reticence, this sorrow that admits no smile,
Only shadow? On my lap the medic's helmet,

Scarred & pitted, white oval for the scarlet cross,
Washed-out colors, fingers toying with the strap.

The wrists, which won't stay folded for the pose,
Are milk-white blurs, as if only my hands could grasp

The details of such inwardness. This time, no caption,
& the ring-less hands will open and clench.

Hands & eyes averted, my image beckons
Then pushes you away.
                              It haunts your desk.

You stare into the glass, your breath against my face
Until our images dissolve—*shadow into light, son into father.*

IV.

Mudlark Shuffle

There too the specialties abounded. The toshers with their lanterns
wade the dawnlit river to their chests, clownish pockets stuffed

with bits of copper, chunks of coal, eight-foot poles
to save themselves should they stumble in some quagmire.

Behind come the mudlarks, children mainly, snatching
from the ooze what the toshers discard. Cabin doors shutting,

iPod on shuffle. Sweet Thames runs softly, on whose banks
Thy gatherers bend to scoop *pure* into their sacks—

dogshit sold to tanners & employed to soften leather.
Bonepickers, dredgermen, nightsoil men, ragmen who might range

thirty miles per day, the Docklands to Hampstead.
A warehouse of bones, a warehouse of pure, a room for clean rags,

another for the soiled. Tray tables upright & the turbines' whir.
A room to die from cholera, a room to perish from consumption.

The specialties abound. The Suit to my right is in finance,
Suit to the left, technology. As we crawl from the gate,

they power down their cells in unison, the ringtone of finance
being the wail of Janis Joplin begging Yahweh for a Benz.

The steward clicks shut his seatbelt lariat & conversation ebbs.
At low tide they'd flock along Blackfriar's Bridge. A mudlark might,

reports Mayhew, earn a penny per day. Beside me columns
shimmer from a laptop. Below, the eggwhite clouds. Finance

grimaces. His friends all drive Porsches & therefore he must
make amends. His cursor glides to Hong Kong. He can't explain

his job in layman's terms. You might find a log to dry
& sell as firewood. Brass buttons & buckles were especially prized.

The mode is shuffle. A digitized Berryman slurs out
Dream Song 29. From a public housing project in Holly Springs,

Mississippi, Junior Kimbrough removes some yearning from himself,
as though by psychic surgery, some foreign object

glistening in his palm & set beside his battered Gibson.
You better run, you better run. Below is Nova Scotia, then

the open water, endless. Finance in a sleep mask & a hundred
tiny screens of BBC, Oscars morphing to a downed plane

in Thailand, wreckage & the crawl above, wreckage & the crawl
below. Into a trance I plummet. Low tide & the fog hangs rank,

pewter swirl against the pilings of the bridge, & the Parliament spires
distant in the dawnlight, blazing. The mud sucks at my boots,

I stumble always bent & watchful. The lanterns of the toshers
firefly the humid soup we wander in, voices of our little multitude,

our Clan of Wander; scan every inch of ground, watchful & bent,
shuffle of my hands as they scoop the ooze, black up to my elbows.

The specialties abound, busily seeking, bob & scoop & bend,
& before me the shine, the glint. Behold the grail of button, o grail

of buckle, grail of a fine ladies' hatpin. A good day; tonight
I will eat. Pry out the star, aglitter in the shit.

Freshwater Bay

Their meat is prized by Yankee whalers
      & thus the beach is strewn with upturned shells,
            Rorschach yellow undersides, weathering against

black sand & too weighty even empty for a man to heft.
      The rowboat glides shoreward, sand so hot
            it melts the soles of Darwin's Wellies, FitzRoy

joking this is but a foretaste of damnation's
      ingenious comeuppances. The tortoises
          have hewn a path up to the spring,

wide & flat enough to manage a hansom
      or a shay. Ponderous & insensible,
          they grope their thoroughfare, FitzRoy

straddling a larger male, who conveys him
      some twenty yards, & only when Darwin
          squats before one, coming level with its eyes,

does it hiss & draw its head in. They count
      two dozen circling the spring, heads below
          the waterline & swallowing

great draughts. Across the sparse grass
      & cacti, a huge old male lumbers toward
          a much smaller female. His cry, notes Darwin,

is long & bassoon-like, a wanton bellow
      that must carry all the way down
          the cliffside to the anchored *Beagle*.

Up her carapace the male creeps, as though pulled
      by some unseen winch. Clangor & the grate
          of shell on shell: the ceremony commences

& shall be longer, Darwin jokes,
      than a Scots Dissenters' camp revival,
          making FitzRoy wince. Bellowing still,

the male flays his huge sienna legs above her shell,
      she paddling farther down into the inky dirt
          so as better to admit him. *So abundant*

is this world, it must beggar the imagination
      even of the Most Omnipotent. FitzRoy
          with his sketchbook hunkers down

to render in charcoal their tectonic amours,
      these antediluvian remnants
          from Creation's dawn, which, he notes

to Darwin—busy jotting in his Moleskine—
      has been shown by Bishop Usher to have
          commenced in 4006 BC.

The yawp & clamor begins anew,
      drowning out Darwin's reply. & by now
          it is twilight. Silent for once,

the men will pick their way down the mountain
      to their skiff & the panoplied leviathans
          will lie together long past moonrise

& the bright ascent of the Southern Cross,
      beneath constellations so alien & various
          they bear no names of heroes, beasts, or gods.

Letter to Eadweard Muybridge

> The subject of the pictures was not the images per se, but the change from one
> to another, the change that represented time and motion.
> —REBECCA SOLNIT

Whiteout, Eadweard. Even the driveway snowblind & within the letters
        of the crawl beneath the screen we watch
the slithering cacophony you set in motion like a railroad baron's thick
        gold watch—school closings first,
then the Buddha's tooth inside a chartered plane, en route to Sri Lanka,
        a camera shaking to more tremors

from Haiti. Car bomb, drone unleashing missile & the doctor who medicated
        the King of Pop to death
is free on bail awaiting trial; he has been enjoined from sedating patients.
        Studies in Motion & before me
the River James in February, bristle of ice floes colliding against the always
        recrudescent Confederacy.

Sleet rides the backs of generals & their Monument stallions, nostrils aflare.
        Jackson, Stuart, dead in battle,
charging northward still. & Lee, heart stopped in his sleep,
        cantering forever South.
Duration, movement, history's blizzard, to which you may be said to lay claim.
        Camera obscura, magic lantern.

Visionary cuckold, lugging your behemoth glass plates to Yosemite
        in a Conestoga train.
You steady your tripod on an outcrop of El Capitán. You shoot
        your wife's lover point blank,
a Colt revolver, the chamber clicking clockwise to permit a second shot.
        Phenakistoscope, Zoopraxiscope.

Occident trots astride your phalanx of cameras, to prove that all four hooves
        have left the ground at once.
Bearded, naked, you yourself stride the camera gauntlet, a guileless
        pilot in an NSA basement, steering a drone

eight thousand miles away. Kandahar below. Coordinates found.
　　　　High-pitched whine as the aircraft hovers.

Then release. Visibility at zero & in a book that asks to be a stream of light,
　　　　Ralph Waldo Emerson declares
he is *part and parcel with God.* The crawl flashes only numbers. I set the book down.
　　　　Tell me of the crawl inside
the crawl, some low unpixelated shimmer to lay these eyes upon,
　　　　like a glimpse of ivory keys.

Zootrope, Faraday Wheel. We are staying tuned, we have forty-two widescreens
　　　　on a gym wall to light our way.
The treadmill beside me nattered on his cell to an AA friend. *You're a stupid*
　　　　fucker if you think that, Frank.
Was she as fucked-up too? Thaumatrope, Choreutoscope. World as chattel,
　　　　possessed of children

chewing *khat* & oiling submachine guns. We cannot step into
　　　　the same crawl twice:
tolls *sans* punctuation, the numbers stagger & exeunt.
　　　　Celebs become dead celebs,
talking on flammable nitrate stock about being alive. A website
　　　　arranges itself—the contents entire

of your *Human Figure in Motion.* Before us stands Robert Connolly,
　　　　The Living Clock, his arms
for twenty-seven years compelled to mimic the minute hand,
　　　　the hour hand. You show him
as 8 o'clock, as 9 o'clock, as 10—O subtle minute hand
　　　　of bone & tendon,

of vascular cat's cradle, of helpless command sputtering
　　　　evermore down the brainstem—
poor man, he "calibrates with uncanny accuracy." Look: the time
　　　　is 11:55, inching
toward 12—the tai chi pose of the hands does not
　　　　distinguish noon from midnight.

In the Domed Stadium

—Houston, TX, after Katrina

Because it's nighttime they have dimmed the lights & now the poor
      must sleep, bobbing their gray
Sargasso of ten thousand cots. A firmament of metal latticework,
      the football pennant constellations.

Groundsmen have rolled up & stored the plastic turf. Next week's
      playoff games & Southeast Texas
Monster Truck Show will go elsewhere, the evangelical crusade
      migrate west to San Diego.

This evening's presidential speech, beamed at them from screens
      six stories high, is over
& the jeering that it brought is done. Exit lights pulse crimson
      & everywhere a twilit shimmer.

Squads of National Guardsmen walk the rows of beds,
      shouldered M-16s,
walkie-talkies sizzling static. & over the low drone of the a/c's hum,
      children sleep two & three

to a cot & the old have folded up their walkers, wallets & dentures
      gripped in their fingers
to protect them from theft. There are crutches, wheelchairs,
      rusted yellow tanks of oxygen

& always the black plastic trashbags, overflowing with clothes
      & toiletries, Gameboys,
Pop Tarts, photo albums of the dead in polyester. The felons
      in their ankle-monitoring devices,

gang tattoos & scars glistening sweat, slumber locked
      & quarantined
inside refreshment stands. The guardsmen pace the rippled sea.
      Some have got the shakes

& some are on the nod. Some have waited hours today
      for antipsychotics
or insulin & others huddle under FEMA blankets, reading
      Stephen King by flashlight.

Three of them will die tonight in sleep & none of them
      will see their homes again.
Here the president will never venture. They would tear him to pieces
      with their hands if they could.

But the means have been found to make them sleep.
      The guardsmen
pace & the poor dream the dreams of the poor,
      though some

still refuse to close their eyes. They are talking
      quietly among themselves,
& the guardsmen, hands twitching beside the stocks of their rifles,
      lean in to hear the conversations.

Nocturne: Newark Airport

> Of what am I guilty?
> —LENI RIEFENSTAHL

Key chains, quarters clinking into plastic trays, shoes off,
snaking belts, laptops spirited from leather cases.

Backpack, stroller, purses boasting Italian monikers,
titanium hip replacements marching

back & forth through detectors—until the TSAers tire
& wave them limping past. To natter

into our cells, to wave our still-corporeal
hands before the automatic sinks. But the ghost dance

is commencing, chains pulled across the stores,
the waxers' hypnagogic back & forth against the tile.

The evidence that we were here is in dispute.
Ochre reddening our mouths, we blow it on the cave wall

through a cattail reed—a stencil of our hands,
often missing fingers. We wander the smoking

ruins of our chancellery. We incise our initials
on the granite feet of Ramses, on Khufu's basalt sarcophagus,

too unwieldy for plunder. We read books
by starlets & millionaires, line up for sushi

& frozen yogurt, reporting tomorrow for a third
tour of duty, rehearsing PowerPoint for the sales convention.

But it's snow from Savannah to Maine;
we'll mill about the gates all night. Big flakes

on smoked glass, mute CNN & its crawl spinning
death tolls. This air we re-breathe

is too much for us. A guardsman bivouacs by a pillar.
The toddlers & their mother sleep

contorted into chairs of plastic & steel.
& I snuggle up with Leni Riefenstahl.

Chamberlain's flown back from Munich,
Leni leaves LA. The Jews of Hollywood

will not recognize her genius, the *honorable exception*
being Walt Disney—who hosts a private screening

of *Snow White*. By midnight the war goes badly, her epic
with its slave labor cast of Gypsies unfinished.

By 1 the OSS arrives, seeking to confirm
that Hitler lacked a testicle. The evidence,

the evidence. Though we are vapor, they will let us
go home; they will decline to prosecute.

They will collect our boarding passes & we'll soar
above the fields & their terrible white monotony.

We will hoist the cameras in our bloodied hands,
photographing sea anemones, the ebony

De Stijl scarification on the backs of Nubian
Warriors. *Brethren, judge therefore yourselves . . .*

Toward dawn now. The mother's head is pillowed
on her jacket, the children fetal

in their chairs. The TV monitor reanimates,
the market in Tokyo is down. Systems check,

we power up. . . . *That ye not be judged.*
The guardsman stirs, another day closer to Helmut Province.

Tracking shot: a pewter sky.
On the runways, the snowplow lights pulse amber.

A Decorated Ghost Dance Shirt

—in memoriam, Jon Anderson

Eagle, magpie, crow: against blue firmament
that boils with hand-sized stars—
                                                    muslin stitched with mocha

elk-hide fringe. You button up the blazing raiment
& for five days you dance, as God's Messenger Wovoka

commands; dance back your peoples from their graves,
dance back the buffalo from their ash pits of bones,

dance paradise earthward—
                                                    each slaughtered tribe
restored. Fever & trance, the auguries unfold.

& the star-bristling shirt is chain-mail, Kevlar
no cavalry bullet can pierce.
                                        I was

Your disciple, Jon. You wore the shirt, the dance
commenced. Glamorous & deluded its

ensorcelating powers. I still know your poems by heart
& yet you died of drink, alone. The star-crossed garment

flutters glass-cased on a wall. A shirt
such as this—who now ever shall don it?

Visiting Dugan

c. 1981

Haze of chain-smoke & I'd come again to show you poems,
        which I understood the first time
was a dubious idea. The magnifying glass was necklaced to your chest.
        Your trembling hand let it
hover the page, syllables pulsing big as highway signs. Next month
        they'd laser at the cataracts,

but now you were lens against lens, horn-rims bulging thick as Waterford Crystal;
        the magnifier hydrofoiled
the turbulent page. Beyond, bright shining flakes of Truro snow
        & beside your desk,
the easel, paper poster-size, permitting you to draft your poems, every letter
        leaden, half slashed through

with marker, the rest unreadable. Comment on Poem the First:
        you used to write better than this.
Poem the Second: *I think I'm getting tired of your parents.* Poem Three:
        Life is shit—always a credible subject—
though you remind me how hard it is to bring off. I ask how your style
        has changed over the years,

between *Poems* & the latest, which at that time would have been
        Poems 6. Writers don't change;
the notion that they do . . . is a capitalist conspiracy. You leave for coffee & a piss,
        damning your fucking prostate,
an organ whose function I had thus far failed to comprehend.
        Cold in the studio,

& a draft is fluttering the easel sheets & the heaps of them
        Knee-high in the corner,
letters massive as the brags that Xerxes hewed into his mountainsides.
        Shyly I rifle through,
hoping to discern the process—one line all in caps per sheet, then thirty or more
        assembled to a draft

that Judy can type up for you. GOD HELP THE FINGERNAILS
          THEY ARE CURSED
BY APATHY   AND ARE NO LONGER CLAWS. How you terrified me.
          & the world, if it knew you
one iota better than it did, would have trembled as well—the factory bosses
          & the CEOs, the heads of PACs,

the radio hosts with their mouths snarling venom. O like the armies of Egypt
          before Alexander, they'd have lain
down their spears & bows to you, heads pressed to the dirt. You're back
          with two mugs, the sheets
still aflutter. *I could only find instant; we're drinking it black.* Those were the days
          I sucked down attention like a long

stiff drink, wholly untutored in gratitude, in the trickeries, betrayals
          & cruelties of the body,
how its provinces rebelled, as Auden who you hated said of Yeats.
          Name a president, you ask,
who was worse than Reagan. Nixon, I say. *Grant, you answer—*
          but the asshole could write.

On the desk you lay open a fat biography. Dying Grant: the cancer that has
          strangled him prohibits speech,
his last words scrawled into a bedside notebook. The characters balloon
          beneath your glass, headline-large
against the failing light. *I do not sleep, though sometimes I doze off a little.*
          If I am up I am talked to

and my efforts cause pain. The fact is I am a verb and not
          a personal pronoun.
A verb is anything that signifies to be, to do, to suffer. I signify all three.
          You let the magnifier dangle.
Pinwheels of snow outside for me, movement occluded & stalled for you.
          Don't worry too much

about the poems, you say, *someday they're bound to get better.*

Web Prayer for Milosz

From euphoria at the blossom's destruction

in time-lapse, save us. We quicken & hiss like serpents,

our tongues flick us forward. We are studies of peritonitis

at the U.S. Forensic Death Farm in Tennessee. From the stunned

half-smiles of the decomposed, we rise. A dwarf inflates

to a giant, bloated like a Macy's float. The corpse

is arranged in Holding Area 232a: the effects

of assault rifle fire have been digitally photographed

for the muse to download for this page, an aggregate of signs

that I have fashioned with her aid. Tell me

to what end, o master. Without you words are pure convention.

Show me where the soul clings on, the Ineffable Name.

The language of the old belief, has it perished?

Keystroke, rictus, click, contusion: the apparitions gather like breath.

Warren Zevon, Johnny Cash

Eleven Nazi doctors prowl Tibet, fashioning

rubber life masks—monks & Sherpas, wailing children.

1937: their quest for the Grail & the Proto-Aryans.

In the dark your second skin grows taut. You enter the spirit realm

& your face is wrenched from your face

by a physical anthropologist from Hamburg

who holds it up for the others to observe.

& then you are vapor, disassembling into space

& borne upon the solar winds, vapor & trophy & nothing else—

no shadow to cast, no longing, a plate of silver gleaming,

squeezing music from my speakers, a snarling affirmation

which survives you & which tells Attila to fuck himself

even as his snow-white stallion rears—boom chucka boom chucka boom

ahhh ooooo—& trods your glorious faces down.

Block Letters

The arrows guide his stroke, pattern
the broken center line to steer along at dawn,

red ochre spit upon a cave wall through a reed,
stenciling a hand.
                    J inverted, *J* erased,

the torso of Adam beckoned from clay, birth-slick,
alluvial & trembling. Fish-hook

of dazzling bone. Small *a* chiseled to high relief—
ramrod spine & nine-month belly of the Venus of Willendorf,

her back to the cricket-thrum of *k*,
the sprinter mid-stride, sharp diagonals. Forward or away?

Ask the Elephant Man: *e* with freakish head,
all cauliflower ear & frontal lobe,

The Great Oz stepping from the curtain, the dry ice oracle.
& he sets down the pencil with a godling smile.

Sepulchre

i.
SOUL

Bury it with rice cakes: these will distract the jackals

guarding the gates of the world below. Bury it

also with a stick to beat them on their muzzles

for often cakes leave them unappeased & hungry are the ghosts

who haunt their way, demanding chattel, cigarettes & money.

Bruise-colored, paltry, rumor has it that its weight

is twenty-one grams. Released, it flutters, a blowfly

alighting, forelegs akimbo, supping on rotted meat. Many-eyed

are its desires, its cravings legion. Clumsy, it waddles,

Baudelaire's albatross, earthbound in its precincts of the flesh.

& then o then does it wail, seeking to dial-up God—

contract & suit, bargain & lobby, pressing

its petition as it looks up from the eating of the softest parts,

incarnadined upon the veldt—sometimes snarling, sometimes in prayer.

ii.

SELF

Is glyph & rune, hammer blow, the Olivetti manual

of D.Y., for nine years clanging by its windowsill

—his lately former dwelling. Is rumored nonexistent save as chattel

& platen, its ribbon special-ordered. Is frontal lobe & pineal,

hammer to silk, anvil-strike to nylon, crinkle of the onionskin

& black demotic, red ink for emphasis, folded like speech for retrieval

by the Next Of Kin. Is Pneuma in the Memory Palace, atoll & agape, rain

in its courtyards, screen doors to further rooms. Acoustic panels,

flammable liquid, Vallejo & Robt. Fripp, electrodes to monitor dreams.

REM-state half-sleep, the heft of several fireflies,

eye-mote & barium, new-moon-with-the-old-moon-in-its-arms.

Samson-self with jawbone of an ass, who slays

three thousand Philistines, soon going hairless & blind. Does not exist

but dwells in rhapsody. One by one by one the keys shall strike.

iii.

SHIT

Symmetry & reformation, centrifuge & loam. "Of the Foure Elementes,

the *plinth* on whiche its breathern rest," of yellow-black earth,

of steppe & prairie. Also its reek, pungent & exact,

which is the dead, is Mother & Father in their vast

mausoleum. Here he pages the *St. Paul Pioneer Press.*

bathroom door ajar in 1950-something, & the stench of it

was Terror & Other. & Mother before her vanity, menses

redolent & tincturing the bedroom while I peer at her. Trite

is the story, but in it we are lost, *selva oscura* & Circle Eight

where the Flatterers wallow in excrement seas.

Grant it then its alchemy, its power & sullen art,

its goldening dead on Judgment Day, ascending from the privies

all corporeal. Behold the grappling hooks, dark ropes uncoiling

to besiege the Holy City—which arises from within.

iv.

SPIRIT

Sunset: you can hear the nighthawks call, wheeling

the garden in their revenant hunger, mist flaring sullen

from the fountain & the lilies' tongues. Walkabout hour, shaman-travelling

down or up into the realm of ghosts. Hour of seance,

phantoms at the turnstile of the medium's throat—

for example my dead Aunt Hope, year of the Missile Crisis,

falsettoing as the table wobbles. Trembling we sat

while the voices cruised in her, hands conjoined as her face

rippled ghostly missives. & now she is among them

as hungry & as chilled, rising into moth-wing, hawk-cry,

voices protoplasmic through my synapses, faintly humming:

cicada hiss & a sparrow bobbing in the fountain, feathers parted by

the maggots craving skin & eye, drilling blind the spirit-gates,

which open for the refugee, hauling his belongings in a cart.

Talismanic

The boys' hair voodoos the tomato stalks.
        We have swept it from the kitchen floor
After haircuts & straw-colored it spirals

    From the garden soil, already half-buried
        Like tablets etched with Linear B,
Untranslatable among eggshells & soap flakes.

        I kneel & watch it rain upon the diligent grubs,

Beetles & the zigzag caravans of ants.
        The stalks nod with unripe Big Boys,
Calypsos, green marbles of Cherries in clusters.

    Human hair, marigolds, Irish Spring
        I flake with a cheese grater in a talismanic
Circle, charms against squirrel & raccoon.

        High summer evening, high 90s & the boys run

Tonsured through the sprinkler spray, the sound
        As it revolves a quirky but robotic
Staccato, like the voice of David Byrne

    Cackling "Once in a Lifetime." *You may ask*
        Yourself, how do I work this?
They will lay waste to the fruits of your labors,

        Useless are all of your spells. For now the wind

Is rising. A thick cheap scent over everything,
        Scent the color of key-lime pie, scent
The color of my father, twenty years dead

& stepping from the shower stall, taking in
        The steam in deep self-conscious
Breaths, his own futile talisman

        Against emphysema, angina, Jim Beam.

Soap lather beards his face. *You may ask yourself,*
        How did I get here? He is ash in a canister
In the Veterans' Cemetery in St. Paul

        & his DNA helixes up the pale outline
        Of Luke's spine, glinting now
In the sprinkler's jittery rainbows. *Let the water*

        Hold me down. Back & forth they pace

The sprinkler's cage. They squeal & turn to me
        In their delight. *Same as it ever was, saamme*
As it ever wassss & the breeze pulls the spray

        Toward me until I am mist as well. Lord,
        Abide this instant back to them when I
Am ash, though I kneel absurdly with

        A cheese grater, kneepads & a flinthead

Of soap. *Same as it e-ver was, same as it*
        e-ver was. Sundown, mosquitoes
tuning up, a gilt of fireflies

        slathering the Adirondack chairs.
        My knees scrape eggshell, beflowered
With deadheaded marigolds, & the tufts of hair

        Billow up from the dirt to my face.

Epigraph to the book: "Shubshi-meshre-Shakkan" is the Babylonian template for the Book of Job. David Ferry's translation appears in *Of No Country I Know: New and Selected Poems and Translations*.

"Scribal": ". . . porcine fascist droning on"—Limbaugh.

"Christ at Emmaus": Van Meegeren has been the subject of several biographies, most recently those of Edward Dolnick and Jonathan Lopez. Dolnick insists that van Meegeren indeed attended the unveiling of his forgery at Museum Boymans; Lopez is less certain. Bakelite, however, was indisputably the forger's secret ingredient. "The greatest Vermeer of all"—a statement by the anonymous art critic of *Time*.

"Self-Portrait Photo of Rimbaud . . .": A reproduction of the photo can be found in Charles Nicholls's *Somebody Else: Arthur Rimbaud in Africa, 1880–91*.

"Rolltop": W. S. Graham's "Lines on Roger Hilton's Watch," *New Collected Poems*.

"Fetish Value": The italicized passages are drawn from Aleda Shirley's *Dark Familiar*.

"Ode to Black 6": The most enduring and successful subspecies of lab mouse, first bred in 1921.

"Jimmie Rodgers's Last Blue Yodel, 1933": See Nolan Porterfield's liner notes to *Jimmie Rodgers 1933: The Last Sessions*—"A cot was set up in the rehearsal hall so that Rodgers could rest from time to time, but he was characteristically impatient with any special attention. When it came time to record, he insisted on standing before the mike as if all was normal."

"For Willy DeVille": Perhaps the greatest and most relentlessly ambitious rock and roll singer you have never heard of. *Le Chat Bleu* (1980) is the best album of a storied *oeuvre*.

"The Apotheosis of Charlie Feathers": The passages of Gnostic scripture derive from James Robinson's *The Nag Hammadi Library*. Feathers is regarded by many as the greatest rockabilly musician, inventor of the widely imitated "hiccupping" vocals found on Elvis's Sun recordings, among others. Feathers went to his death believing Sun founder Sam Phillips had cheated him of fame and fortune. Feathers's best recordings can be found on *Get With It: Essential Recordings 1954–69.*

"World Tree": In the closing paragraphs of his classic study *Shamanism: Archaic Techniques of Ecstasy,* Eliade writes, "It is likewise probable that pre-ecstatic euphoria constituted one of the universal sources of lyric poetry. In preparing his trance, the shaman drums, summons his spirit helpers, speaks 'a secret language' or 'the animal language,' imitating the cries of beasts and especially the songs of birds. He ends by obtaining a 'second state' which provides the impetus for linguistic creation and the rhythms of lyric poetry. Poetic creation still remains an act of perfect spiritual freedom. Poetry remakes and prolongs language; every poetic language begins by being a secret language, that is, the creation of a personal universe . . ." The Cash/Strummer rendition of Marley's "Redemption Song" can be found on the posthumously issued *Cash Unearthed.*

"Ochre": sources for this sequence include Sarah Greenough, Diane Waggoner, et al., *The Art of the American Snapshot 1888–1978;* Clement Cheroux, Andres Fischer, et. al., *The Perfect Medium: Photography and the Occult;* Jule Eisenbud, *The World of Ted Serios;* Jean Clottes, *Chauvet Cave: The Art of Earliest Times;* Gregory Curtis, *The Cave Painters;* Gustaf Sobin, *Luminous Debris;* Steven Mithen, *After the Ice: A Global Human History, 20,000–5,000 BC;* Alexander Marshack, *The Roots of Civilization;* Peter Goodchild, *J. Robert Oppenheimer;* Jane Mayer, *The Dark Side.* I owe thanks to Mary Flinn, Greg Donovan, Emilia Philips, David Freed, and especially Robert Jackson, whose great collection of snapshots inspired the sequence, and Tristan Kerr, for his masterful renderings of the Neolithic artworks. Thanks are also due to the *Blackbird* staff for their work on the project, especially Michael Keller, Patrick Scott Vickers, Grant White, Tony Marshall, Randy Marshall, and Gregory Kimbrell, as well as to the National Gallery of Art and Deputy Director and Chief Curator Franklin Kelly. The image called "Photograph of Colonel Allerton S. Cushman and His Wife with the Spirit of Agnes, Their Deceased Daughter, 24 July 1921," is reprinted from the Archives of the American Society for Psychical Research with the permission of the American Society for Psychical Research, Inc. (ASPR), 5 West 73rd Street, New York, New York, 10023, www.aspr.com, aspr@aspr.com. The sequence is dedicated to Jean Valentine.